SONGS FOR RELINQUISHING THE EARTH

SONGS FOR RELINQUISHING THE EARTH

Jan Zwicky

Brick Books

Canadian Cataloguing in Publication Data

Zwicky, Jan, 1955–
   Songs for relinquishing the earth

Poems.

ISBN 1-894078-00-4

I. Title.

PS8599.W53S66 1998   C811'.54   C98-932237-8
PR9199.3.Z94S66 1998

We acknowledge the support of the Canada Council
for the Arts for our publishing programme. The
support of the Ontario Arts Council is also gratefully
acknowledged.

This book is set in Diotima, designed by
Gudrun Zapf-von Hesse, as interpreted by
the electronic type foundry of Adobe Systems.

Design: Sally McKay and Jan Zwicky

Layout: Sally McKay

Printed on recycled stock and bound by
Sunville Printco Inc.

Brick Books
431 Boler Road, Box 20081
London, Ontario N6K 4G6
email: brick.books@sympatico.ca

SONGS FOR RELINQUISHING THE EARTH

A Note on the Text	7
Open Strings	9
Bartók's Roumanian Dances	11
K. 219, Adagio	12
Brahms' Clarinet Quintet in B Minor, Op. 115	13
Bill Evans: "Here's That Rainy Day"	14
Bill Evans: *Alone*	15
Musicians	16
Kant and Bruckner: Twelve Variations	17
The Geology of Norway	32
Transparence	37
Cashion Bridge	41
Five Songs for Relinquishing the Earth	49
Border Station	54
Poppies	56
Recovery	57
Shade	58
Beethoven: Op. 95	60
Beethoven: Op. 127, Adagio	67
Absence	70
Lancey Meadows	71
The View from the Kitchen Window	72
April	73
Rain Shadow	74
Highway 879	75
You Must Believe in Spring	76
Lilacs	78
Driving Northwest	80
Passing Sangudo	81
Trauermusik	83

A Note on the Text

Songs for Relinquishing the Earth was first published by the author in 1996 as a hand-made book, each copy individually sewn for its reader in response to a request. It appeared between plain covers on recycled stock, with a small photo (of lavender fields) pasted into each copy. The only publicity was word of mouth.

Part of Jan Zwicky's reason for having the author be the maker and distributor of the book was a desire to connect the acts of publication and publicity with the initial act of composition, to have a book whose public gestures were in keeping with the intimacy of the art. She also believed the potential audience was small enough that she could easily sew enough copies to fill requests as they came in. While succeeding in recalling poetry's public life to its roots, she was wrong about the size of that audience and her ability to keep up with demand as word spread. Hence, this facsimile edition. In publishing it, Brick Books has attempted to remain as faithful as possible to the spirit of those original gestures, while making it possible for more readers to have access to this remarkable book.

Open Strings

E, laser of the ear, ear's
vinegar, bagpipes
in a tux, the sky's blue, pointed;

A, youngest of the four, cocksure
and vulnerable, the white kid
on the basketball team — immature,
ambitious, charming,
indispensable; apprenticed
to desire;

D is the tailor
who sewed the note "I shall always love you"
into the hem of the village belle's wedding dress,
a note not discovered until ten years later in New York
where, poor and abandoned, she was ripping up the skirt
for curtains, and he came,
and he married her;

G, cathedral of the breastbone,
oak-light, earth;

it's air they offer us,
but not the cool draught of their half-brothers
the harmonics, no,
a bigger wind, the body
snapped out like a towel, air
like the sky above the foothills,
like the desire to drown,

a place of worship,
a laying down of arms.
                              Open strings
are ambassadors from the republic of silence.
They are the name of that moment when you realize
clearly, for the first time,
you will die. After illness,
the first startled breath.

Bartók's Roumanian Dances

Arranged for old French organ: an idea
with the market savvy of the Edsel.
In the last twenty seconds, in a fury
the organist yanks out a bird stop, twittering,
yodelling, Don Cherry crossed with a chickadee, a polka
for demented gargoyles, our dead dog, our dying friend, I can't
leave the house to mail a letter without thinking
it could be the last time I see you.

It's a coin, this craziness, this
beauty. Goldenrod, prodigal with light
beside the pebbly stream, the car, the car radio,
the concrete balustrade, wind
slapping my face, the carrot tops flapping
in the paper bag beside me on the seat, all of it, every
particle, unbearable. And Bartók
starving in his New York kitchen, the
spoons, the pots. And lungs drawing breath,
feet kicking rhythm, the body
headlong in its worship of the air,
or the air,
which is boundless and momentary.

K. 219, Adagio

Now the sky above New Mexico
is hazy with Los Angeles, what words
will you invent for clarity?

Some things were always nameless:
the heart as rainbarrel,
the ear a long-stemmed glass.

The fiddle is still maple tuned with starlight,
the bow, breath with a backbone,
sweet with sap.

That long trill
is a hand that lifts your hair
a final time, sunlight, a last kiss

that knows it is the last.
And the phrase that follows:
a small voice talking to itself, how

some moments are so huge
you notice only little things:
nicks in the tabletop, the angle of a fork.

Drink. It
is what you will have
to remember:

rain's vowelless syntax,
how mathematics was an elegy,
the slenderness of trees.

Brahms' Clarinet Quintet in B Minor, Op. 115

That we shall not forget to honour
brown, its reedy clarities.

And, though the earth is dying
and the names of its diseases
spread from the fencelines, Latinate:
a bright field
ribboned with swath.

That the mind's light could be filtered
as: a porch, late afternoon,
a trellised rose,
                    which is to say
a truth in nostalgia:
if we steel ourselves against regret
we will not grow more graceful,
but less.

That a letter might honestly
begin, *Dear beloved*.

Bill Evans: "Here's That Rainy Day"

On a bad day, you come in from the weather
and lean your back against the door.
This time of year it's dark by five.
Your armchair, empty in its pool of light.

That arpeggio lifts, like warmth, from the fifth of B minor,
offers its hand — *let me*
tell you a story . . . But in the same breath,
semitones falling to the tonic:
you must believe and not believe;
that door you came in
you must go out again.

In the forest, the woodcutter's son
sets the stone down from his sack and speaks to it.
And from nothing, a spring wells
falling as it rises, spilling out
across the dark green moss.
There is sadness in the world, it says,
past telling. Learn stillness
if you would run clear.

Bill Evans: *Alone*

Sound that makes night fall around it
like the glow from a reading lamp.

Rain on the roof, straight down.
The name of your name
spoken without another's.

Rubato is a hand
you thought indifferent
laid, briefest of moments,
on your sleeve.

It walks away, then,
that sound, without looking back.
Lights up a Lucky. Says

we hadn't the ghost of a chance, says never
let me go.

Musicians

I pass a bunch of musicians in the street.
It's about 12:30, rehearsal just over, they're
standing around outside the side door of the church.
A good rehearsal; and it's April. They're laughing,
horsing around, talking about shoes, or taxes, where
to go for lunch, anything
except what their heads are full of.
It's a kind of helplessness, you can see
they're still breathing almost in unison, like people
the searchlight has passed over
and spared, their attention
lifts, swerves, settles; even
the gravel dust stuttering at their feet
is coherent.

Kant and Bruckner: Twelve Variations

The set of variations that follows grows out of a long-standing conviction that the number and *sort* of echoes in the lives of Immanuel Kant and Anton Bruckner have to be more than coincidental. Not least striking among the correspondences is the fact that there are few biographies of either, those that exist are slim, and many open with apologies for the 'boring' character of their subjects' lives. — Yet the lives were extraordinary. Neither man produced much of anything until middle or late-middle age, and then what each produced was massive: dense, huge, and astonishingly intricate. Both were, by contrast with their work, naïfs: devoutly religious, devoted to their mothers, anxious not to offend. Both were virgins, although apparently heterosexual; and eccentric: — Bruckner liked to go around looking at people's corpses, and tried to collect as many certificates of competence as he could get people to examine him for. Kant ate one meal a day, at one o'clock, which was always attended by guests he had had his manservant invite that morning; he was renowned as a conversationalist, possibly in part because he believed one had a moral duty to tell genuinely funny after-dinner jokes, laughter being an aid to digestion. The housewives of Königsberg set their clocks by his daily walk — a solitary walk, as Kant had some unusual notions about the transmission of germs.

Kant didn't like music, except for brass bands — the basis of Bruckner's orchestral palette. Both were early risers (Bruckner wrote a fugue every morning before breakfast) and extremely popular as teachers. Both were obsessive revisers. Although the documentation is not very explicit, it appears that Bruckner had a nervous breakdown during which his numeromaniac tendencies became very pronounced. His own instruments were the country fiddle, and the organ. On the latter, he was one of the century's great virtuosi, though he wrote little music for it, preferring to improvise in concert. His favourite musical interval, the key to the architectonic of his symphonies and masses, is the semi-tone. Despite its chromaticism, however, his music remains profoundly diatonic in organization and inspiration.

At the centre of Kant's thought is his debate with Hume, whose skeptical arguments concerning the nature of our apprehension of causal relations, Kant tells us, first interrupted his 'dogmatic slumber'. By the time he was fully awake, Kant had extended the scope of the discussion to embrace much of the history of modern western European philosophy. Kant's Transcendental Deduction aims, among other things, to hook the solipsistic interior that idealism gives us back up to the real world. If it fails, then the skeptics are right: we can't get from 'in here' to 'out there' (or to there even being an 'out there') by rational reflection alone. And this, of course, would make for some serious problems in a discipline defined by the thought that 'to know' means 'to know rationally'.

Bruckner had career troubles of his own. His work was frequently the object of savage attacks by the powerful Viennese critic, Eduard Hanslick. In the hopes of reconciling Hanslick to Bruckner, Bruckner's friends arranged a meeting — but Bruckner was so nervous, he was unable to enter the building where Hanslick was waiting for him. Even after many years in Vienna, his manners retained an old-fashioned and provincial cast, and to the end of his life, he was regarded by Viennese society as something of a country bumpkin. He was, in addition, absent-minded, and is reported on at least one crucial occasion to have worn mismatched socks.

Material in italics in Variation 7 is taken from Norman Kemp Smith's translation of the first *Critique*. The quotation in Variation 5 is from Scruton's biographical sketch at the beginning of his book, *Kant*. The Latin in Variation 2 is a tag from Virgil, Kant's favourite poet: 'They keep out of the hives the drones, an indolent bunch' (*Georgics* IV, 168). Kant quotes it at the conclusion of the Preface to the *Prolegomena*, using it to commend 'sound critical principles'. His view is that difficult and obscure though the *Critique* may seem in places, the project of modern metaphysics stands or falls with the comprehension of its arguments. This is not, in my view, an exaggerated assessment.

The voice, to use a highfalutin term, is polyphonic — it moves around a lot. Sometimes it is Kant's, sometimes Bruckner's, sometimes that of both, sometimes that of an observer. Among the observer-voices, there is one that deserves special mention in connection with the conventions governing the composition of sets of classical variations. Not infrequently, especially in the works of Haydn and Beethoven, the sublime and the ridiculous are deliberately juxtaposed — the meditative tension is relieved by a scherzo. This goofing-off usually occurs about two-thirds or three-quarters of the way through. It appears here in Variation 8.

*

What did they want of me?
What's worth saying?

A terrible thing, always losing your socks.
God is everywhere, everywhere.

This is the shortest path:
there is only one. Listen.

Clouds above the western mountains;
a good laugh.

Close your eyes. Not what you knew then.
Not even what you know now.

If reason cannot do it, what then?
Don't care for music, never have.

How is pure math possible? Turn inward: you will
see the left hand's glove can never fit the right.

Love your mother. Love the moral law,
the path up and the path down. *Lieber Gott,*

we cannot touch a hair
without affecting all the rest.

Bees of the invisible. *Ignavum
fucos pecus a praesepibus arcent.*

Gesture unhurried.
The shoe that's on the right foot

will not fit the left.
The way is clear.

Organ lofts: in Linz, Kremsmünster, Steyr.
If the practice is coherent, we are free.

Improvise! St. Epvre, the Crystal Palace, Notre Dame: there's
                                                    Bach
for those who need to see it written down.

Step by step, semitone by semitone.
The bishop, listening, too moved to pray.

Schönberg will be wrong. Yes, even now
it's everywhere and every second

thundering, erupting home. Hume saw.
Without synthetic a priori,

we are lost. The *size* of it!
You think the Dutch might understand?

A rainbow arched across the canyon. Bridge
of stone. No wonder you are blind.

Something brushes past your head.
God's claw.

A terrible thing, always losing your socks.
Scratches on the handles of the bureau drawer.

Mass in D Minor: 40 years old. *Critique*
of Pure Reason: 57. Lively lecture styles.

You can determine everything. Or nothing.
What's to tell? "His blameless life . . . "

The path has no algebra. Its geometry
is perfect.

Walk alone. Breathe through your nose.
Converse with no one out of doors.

One meal a day at, exactly, one. Death's face
is numberless and duty means a good joke.

Static, they say, and repetitious; set
your clock; but look, they haven't seen what I have:

it's the size of Texas! *Listen*:
safety lies in numbers. *Sicherheit*

and certainty. Oh father, count them,
count them! — stars, leaves, pearls, the Danube

swelling, flashing, thundering and plunging,
glittering, it swallows us.

A good laugh aids digestion. Add
the practical necessity of freedom

and you get a knock-down argument
for telling after-dinner jokes. Yet

the soul, like noumena,
unknowable —

out past the last outpost of reason.
We yet comprehend *it is*

incomprehensible. Open the door.
Sunlight and singing. *All that we may ask.*

"Forms of intuition", "categories
of the understanding" — nah,

forget the prose: the argument's
built like a Rolls. That Hume, see,

he weren't taken with the view, so
when the rad blew,

quit. Thing was, he saw you just can't get
from here to there by car.

(Walked out with his pool cue, so they say.
Don't meet a mind like his just every day.)

The pale brown of the lilac hedge grows paler.
Tinier and tinier, the stitches in the quilt.

Finches, too: a singular array
on the pocked February snow. It's all

you see, or nothing.
Hume, that acute man.

A fugue a day keeps god's
claws at bay. Routine

can render one invisible. It's true.
There's no place safe.

We *have* searched, sir. No sign
of early talent, never could conduct. His first

Beethoven concert failed to stand him
on his ear. (In Linz, sir; No. 4; apparently

a fine performance.) Couldn't sight read. Desperate
for approval (quite pathetic, really, sir) but

never thought to mend his overcoat. Wore baggy pants,
liked sauerkraut. Numeromaniac. A virgin.

Nothing else, sir. We're afraid
that's it.

What did they want of me?
Terror, beauty, heaven, and the moral

law; the angels' hot chromatic breath.
Or symphonies, critique unfurling

like an amaryllis on its leafless stalk.
I've seen Beethoven's corpse, believe me

genius will not save you. Schönberg
will be wrong. But Hume?

God's hand in the bureau drawer:
one sock, two sock, red sock, blue sock.

Rainbow arch of stone across the canyon.
Sun cascading through the pass.

Water, light: that's the shape of it:
silence.

Love the countryside. Your mother.
Brass bands. Exactitude.

It's not about music or ideas.
We both knew you couldn't be too careful.

Close your eyes.
The bridge is exactly as wide as your foot.

The Geology of Norway

But when his last night in Norway came, on 10 December, he greeted it with some relief, writing that it was perfectly possible that he would never return.
— Ray Monk, *Ludwig Wittgenstein*

I have wanted there to be
no story. I have wanted
only facts. At any given point in time
there cannot be a story: time,
except as now, does not exist.
A given point in space
is the compression of desire. The difference
between this point and some place else
is a matter of degree.
This is what compression is: a geologic epoch
rendered to a slice of rock you hold between
your finger and your thumb.
That is a fact.
Stories are merely theories. Theories
are dreams.
A dream
is a carving knife
and the scar it opens in the world
is history.
The process of compression gives off thought.
I have wanted
the geology of light.

They tell me despair is a sin.
I believe them.
The hand moving is the hand thinking,
and despair says the body does not exist.
Something to do with bellies and fingers

pressing gut to ebony,
thumbs on keys. Even the hand
writing is the hand thinking. I wanted
speech like diamond because I knew
that music meant too much.

And the fact is, the earth is not a perfect sphere.
And the fact is, it is half-liquid.
And the fact is there are gravitational anomalies. The continents
congeal, and crack, and float like scum on cooling custard.
And the fact is,
the fact is,
and you might think the fact is
we will never get to the bottom of it,
but you would be wrong.
There is a solid inner core.
Fifteen hundred miles across, iron alloy,
the pressure on each square inch of its heart
is nearly thirty thousand tons.
That's what I wanted:
words made of that: language
that could bend light.

Evil is not darkness,
it is noise. It crowds out possibility,
which is to say
it crowds out silence.
History is full of it, it says
that no one listens.

The sound of wind in leaves,
that was what puzzled me, it took me years
to understand that it was music.
Into silence, a gesture.
A sentence: that it speaks.
This is the mystery: meaning.
Not that these folds of rock exist
but that their beauty, here,
now, nails us to the sky.

The afternoon blue light in the fjord.
Did I tell you
I can understand the villagers?
Being, I have come to think,
is music; or perhaps
it's silence. I cannot say.
Love, I'm pretty sure,
is light.
              You know, it isn't
what I came for, this bewilderment
by beauty. I came
to find a word, the perfect
syllable, to make it reach up,
grab meaning by the throat
and squeeze it till it spoke to me.
How else to anchor
memory? I wanted language
to hold me still, to be a rock,
I wanted to become a rock myself. I thought

if I could find, and say,
the perfect word, I'd nail
mind to the world, and find
release.
The hand moving is the hand thinking:
what I didn't know: even the continents
have no place but earth.

These mountains: once higher
than the Himalayas. Formed in the pucker
of a supercontinental kiss, when Europe
floated south of the equator
and you could hike from Norway
down through Greenland to the peaks
of Appalachia. Before Iceland existed.
Before the Mediterranean
evaporated. Before it filled again.
Before the Rockies were dreamt of.
And before these mountains,
the rock raised in them
chewed by ice that snowed from water
in which no fish had swum. And before that ice,
the almost speechless stretch of the Precambrian:
two billion years, the planet
swathed in air that had no oxygen, the Baltic Shield
older, they think, than life.

So I was wrong.
This doesn't mean
that meaning is a bluff.
History, that's what
confuses us. Time
is not linear, but it's real.
The rock beneath us drifts,
and will, until the slow cacophony of magma
cools and locks the continents in place.
Then weather, light,
and gravity
will be the only things that move.

And will they understand?
Will they have a name for us? — Those
perfect changeless plains,
those deserts,
the beach that was this mountain,
and the tide that rolls for miles across
its vacant slope.

Transparence

Do not drink
the darkness, said Pythagoras,
the soul cannot become pure darkness.
— Robert Bringhurst

I would reply to Pythagoras
nor can the soul
become pure light.

Or if it does, the experience,
unless you are freakishly lucky — like
that woman, thrown from her car, her car
rolling and bouncing up one side of the embankment and then
back down, to land on top of her, except
the roof had been dented by the guardrail
and it came down with the hollow
over her and she escaped
unscathed — will kill you.

So we are caught stumbling
in between, longing for home.

*

Things we leave behind: the belief
that nothing else will matter as much again,
and this: if we could learn
to let go without leaving then
our real lives might begin.

Where do we hang our hats? Up the long slope
we are always running to in dreams?

Or here, in the confused kitchen of paychecks
and good intentions, one black one
double-double, make that to go? Meaning
is a measure of resistance: to that hand
shoving you out over the cliff of your future,
to the thought of your own hands
gulping for the substance of the familiar. And
nothing *will* matter as much
as those back stairs, that red bench,
the Matisse drawing cut from a calendar
years ago, left curling on the garage wall
after the yard sale, remembered suddenly
with vividness just west of Oshawa.
Something not a bone
but like a bone — just here, behind the clutter
in your chest — broken so many times
it's ground to dust; and you bend, resistless,
to shoulder every absence.

*

Light lives
everywhere: no legs, no breath,
no need for shoes. Its unmoorings
effortless, nothing
in tow. No need
for hands: it does not take itself
to be responsible. Light
carries nothing, and the place
it thinks, it is.

*

Mornings after rain, the mind wakes
dewy, tender — bad news, miscalculations
piled behind it like a shelf of badly-folded blankets.
Only in fairy tales,
or given freakish luck, does the wind
rise suddenly and set you down where everything
is safe and loved and in its place. The mind
does not expect it. But the heart,
                                   the heart —
the heart keeps looking for itself.
It knows and does not know
where it belongs. It quivers
like a compass, taut with anticipation,
the sweet thump
of arrival. The heart,
a solid thing, is dark
like turf, and it believes
luck is a talent, or a form of light —
at least, its due for service —
and refuses to be schooled.

*

Dust from the eighteen-wheeler
whipping in to the Dryden Husky as we
step out of the restaurant — it looks like fog —
and I'm reminded of the morning river-mists

in the scrub parkland where I grew up,
walking through them how they'd swirl,
evaporate, the dampness on the grass
sighed into sky. Here in August,
northern Ontario, evening,
grit sticks to my face and neck, sits in my lungs.
Out of sight, the rig door slams and someone laughs.
I spill my coffee as I struggle with the lid.
As we pull away
the dust's still there, sun
catching it, and being caught,
exactly: a lightness you can see
right through, suspended
in the night-blue air.

Cashion Bridge

It would be as well at the outset to admit
how even to have said this much
is to have failed. That the moment that I want to slow into slow-
                                                    motion,
hold up to the light, not in stop-time but in the starry leak of
                                        epochs, the light
that floats in the apse of Salisbury, that ebbs north from Churchill in
                                                    October,
the light that dark remembers,
has already passed. In that light, this moment:
hands poised above the keys, bow at the apex of its arc toward the
                                                    string
— last night someone was coughing, my neighbour
shifted in his seat — but it was that moment
that we'd come for, the one
most full of silence, fingers stretching through it to —
                                        well,
what? the piece? the *thing*?
                        — but by then, the light's
snapped on, the note has flashed and risen
like the downstroke of the nib, dawn slicing the horizon,
the paddle breaking through the surface, scarring it
with light. Hegel wrote:
not curiosity, not vanity,
not the consideration of expedience, not duty or conscience
but an unquenchable unhappy thirst that brooks no compromise
leads us to truth. He also wrote:
only by understanding what it's not
can we come to understand what something is.
This is the difficulty of beginnings.

You are walking west.
The elderberry's turned, and some branches of the maples at
Kennedy's
are bronze: the colour's dull this year because of drought.
The Glover's new canes have come on, though —
just enough rain at the right time; earlier
they lost the old canes and the crop.
Old Mr. Irvine's lane, Dave Petepiece's,
then his brothers' driveways: their mother died
last month: looks like, out back,
someone is learning how to drive.
The stretch down the far side of the rise, scotch pine
and two oaks on the north, a maple on the south,
people we don't know in the place set back from the road.
Up the next rise, Spillers, new,
from Montreal, and the people with the big dog
on the right. The blank unwindowed barn —
and odourless — along the left. Then
cornfields; more cornfields; and the shingle-sided shack,
we don't know who, red window-frames and plastic on the
windows,
and you're at the Cashion sideroad.
South
takes you to the swamp — the unofficial
dump — and then across abandoned tracks
down to the Glen: narrow, bush-lined, not kept up, much
used
by traffickers in U.S. contraband.
North, the sideroad's wider;
white with gravel, though I've never met a car.
An open field of corn on the east side, and on the west
a meadow, heavy with alsike and alfalfa,

and a hardwood bush that rises on the fencelines to the west
                                        and north;
  in fact, the last few hundred feet you walk through shade
  after mid-day, though I don't know how far west
  the patch of trees extends: as far as you can see, from the bridge,
  but the river bends just upstream
  and it's hard to tell.

But this isn't
what I meant to try to say:
it's the starting out
I do not understand.
Years earlier, after midnight in a different province,
the gravel drops away in front of us. You can smell
the water: *Lights Off*
While Waiting For The Ferry: but no red-green
wink to say they've seen us from the other side: windows down,
a transport passing on the highway back of us, reeds
shifting slightly in the breeze,
then still again.
We flick our lights.
No shout, no quiver in the tow line,
just the little ridge of stones and sand shoved up
where the ramp has butted on the shore.
It's hard to give up — the town we live in visible, just there,
but forty minutes by the nearest bridge;
exhaustion hours old.
One sees with the greatest clarity,
sees nothing.

            I don't know
how many times I've walked to Cashion Bridge.

There are other lovely walks, of course,
and often I will wander east, or south,
or off along the tracks to town.
But this is my favourite. It's odd I've never
set foot on the other side; though I've noticed
you can hear, or even in the distance see,
the flit of cars or half-tons on the South Branch.
I miss the old boards: this version of the bridge
is new, they built it now a few years back.
The concrete gleams, white like the gravel,
where it's not in shade. I sit
by the drain, against the balustrade along the west.
A frog or turtle drops into the water
under me, among the reeds. A clump of perfect cat-tails,
three straight and two a little bowed. The willows stretching out
                                        across the water,
currentless and brown.
                       But this isn't
what I meant to tell you either. What I wanted
was the walking, not the walking-to but
the not-getting-there, the every moment
starting out, the every moment
being lifted in an arc against the moment of arrival: the anticipation
is terrific, yet always nothing
happens when I'm there — so
not even this, but the ungraspableness
of knowing, the inarticulateness of
that flexed second above the keys,
of how we are translated,
                       that held breath
between the future and the past that's neither, but is still

the only place we'll ever be arriving
to, the only place it's possible
we are.

       Five o'clock on a rainy day.
Waking, with suddenness, to the open window.
Almost, you remember what it was like
when the future was ahead of you,
when the distant sound of the highway through the wet leaves
was the sound of a world
being invented.
           Yesterday,
on the radio, Bruckner's Second, clearing up the stuff from lunch
and there it was: the image of existence
being wrung out like a dishcloth in those chords, that
torqued crazy counterpoint, the name
of something language wants but cannot find the words
to say, that mash of semitones
the echo of the pressure from the other side,
the everything that what is isn't, its brink
the outline of the moment
of the hands above the keys — I think of Bruckner
walking that knife-edge
singing, and I am inclined
      to meet my class in rags, I am inclined
      to break down in the street,
      to wish for hurricanes,
      I am inclined to write my friends on placemats from the
                           Chinese take-out,
      to tell someone, anyone, what I really think.
So we might begin.

That room you've
lived in summers, from which you've started out:
the chair sits, turned a little sideways from the desk,
in silence now. The window
closed. Light falls through the curtains:
it is dust. Each day
the air grows imperceptibly more still
and cold.
                    What is this, that looks
so much like loyalty? Thinking that the future, your return,
will give this present meaning
is just one more gesture of possession: imagining
the emptiness as loss, as failure, a stutter
in the pure trajectory of occupation — no, what I mean is
yes, it is a failure, of course it's failure,
but not the one we think it is.
                              For that is what
the world has been: not
what we thought.
Kant, Hegel, Heidegger,
the ghosts of Descartes — thinking
we are being's origin
is trying to become
its end. Bruckner was right: the world
is always letting go, it is
the moment of the hands above the keys,
the silence of beginning.
On the bridge, sun stammering through the willow leaves,
                                        white,
yellow, gold, is the futureless unnarrative of light, the every
                                        moment
starting out, staring straight up into it, being stared into,
fiery, hammering, light like trumpets, the cells

of your body alight, your mouth
open and disintegrating.
                                          That last afternoon
we drove in the opposite direction — east first, then crossed
the Raisin at the Glenbrook bridge,
hauling thirty years, five families, from the attic and the cellar
to the township dump. Abandoning it there
at the lip of that huge scree
the way we know the world
will soon abandon us. But the world
knows otherwise: knows
even history is merely mortal,
and that the shrugging-off of ownership is other than
the letting-go of love, which is every moment turning from
the green translucent garden hose, the box of bathroom tiles,
the beauty of the comic books and drawers of kitchen clutter: corks,
          sealer lids, can-openers, bent straws and butter knives;
the lawnchair webbing, and the lawnchair frames, torn mattresses
          and bedsteads, the beauty of the plastic kitchen chairs;
a lampshade with pressed forget-me-not's and pansies,
wicker plantstands, birdfeeders, the Encyclopaedia Brittanica *Dama to*
          Educ and *Text to Vasc*, the complete symphonies of Beethoven,
a rubber boot, stoves, fridges, eavestroughing, roll-up blinds, end
          tables, tires, their beauty, shingles,
stuff in jars; and the beauty of dead trees, loose cushions and a box
          of 1922 Ontario Readers, the beauty
of jumbles of clothesline, broken cinder block, barbed wire coils and
                                          television aerials,
of two pots without their lids, a pink blanket, gas cans, stuffed toys
                                          and bedsprings;
of the sea of garbage bags, the bobbing green, black, blue, and orange
                                          garbage bags;

and boxes of shirts and sweaters, trousers, rags, unrecyclable plastic:
                                                        sheets
crumpled in the mass of things; bleach bottles, rolls of wall-to-wall;
the beauty of the chesterfields with matching chairs, the leather
        Lazyboy with stuffing coming out its arm,
the sheen on the stacks of rotting newsprint, phonebooks, velvet paint-
        by-number sets; the broken patio umbrella, children's bicycles;
and the bits of dowelling, radiant, the broken quarter round and
        two-by-fours with peeling paint, the gleam
of momentariness, throat raised, the knife edge
incandescent with its failure, knowing itself failed,
and singing.

Five Songs for Relinquishing the Earth

The rock weeps into its own whiteness.
Sunny meadow slopes, the gentians,
     far above.
The sun, too, tumbles down. A symphony
of spruce boughs sinks into the fiery moss.

Jewel-music, the amber roar of the falls.
No one thinks of home.
Waiting in the cool shadows,
we are dappled with hope.

Remember how the track swung out
around the cutbank in the full light of noon?
In my dream,

I took off my rings then, my bracelets,
        the gold locket.
To stand bare-headed among the pines!

The fascination of water
is the laughter of geometry.
Wind plunges down the hillside:
        a longing to embrace.

The mountain drifts in twilight.
When we draw the blinds at dusk
is the moment we most want to open
        them again.

Delicacy of mule deer, the sharp
           dry scent of spruce —
we have been grateful for the smallest kindnesses:
a shelf that holds up books, dry socks.

Rain streaks the windows of the cabin.
Of course, the earth once moved
           on fragile stilts like theirs.
Thought rolls down a crack, is lost.

A sky with holes, a desert
           in the Amazon,
you, black stump, rigid in slash: —
Mist writhes from the surface of the lake.

We are tired.
The wooden bowl is empty.
All night, arguments with strangers, dim
           corridors, panic.

It is spring. The gullies are dry.
One makes camp in a rocky meadow
       under a plain of stars.

The hands fold themselves in sleep then;
and the ears, the eyes; the tongue
       in its dark cavern.
The mind walks alone to the horizon.

When it returns, its face will be white,
the compass will lie broken
       in its broken hand.

And when the tent flap flutters
in the windy dawn, where the heart lay
       will be nothing.

Border Station

There had been flooding all that summer, I recall,
acres of grey-brown footage from the Midwest —
but with reports confined to property, and human interest,
the reasons for the land's incontinence suppressed, those images
had skimmed past, seeming, as usual, not quite real.
The day had been hot, clear,
we'd eaten supper on the porch, and
later, quite late, had turned the radio on upstairs —
some thought of midnight news, perhaps —
I don't remember now.
The signal we pulled in — strongly,
because we weren't far from the border then —
was the last half-hour of a Brewers-Red Sox game.
It was coming from Milwaukee,
top of the ninth, two out, the Brewers leading,
and we hadn't been listening long when the announcer,
between a line out and Hatcher's
coming to the plate, commented on the weather:
there'd been a rain delay, it had been raining heavily before,
but now was easing up, just a light shower falling,
though a lot of lightning was still visible to the east and south.
Raised on the prairies, I
could see it clearly, suddenly
could see the whole scene clearly:
the crowd dwindling, several
umbrellas, the glittering aluminum of vacated seats,
the misted loaf of arc-lit light, the night,
deeper by contrast, thick and wet and brown
around it, flickering.

And at the same time I was struck, too — like
looking out across a huge relief map — by the hundreds of miles
between our bedroom and Milwaukee, by that continental
distance, and was overtaken inexplicably
by sorrow.
                    It was as though
in that moment of deep focus
I had tasted the idea of America.
As though it really might have had
something to do with baseball, and radio, and the beauty
of the storms that can form in the vast light above the plains — or,
no, extremity of some kind — clarity, or tenderness —
as though, that close to the end, levels
already rising on the leveed banks again,
the mistakes might have been human:
not justifiable, but as though
some sort of story might be told, simply,
from defeat, without apology, the way you might describe
the fatal accident — not to make sense of it,
but just to say, too late but still to say,
something had happened:
there was blood, blood everywhere, we hadn't realized,
by the time we noticed, rivers of it,
nothing could be done.

Poppies

Some days, the wall that separates us from the future
is too thin. Standing in my mother's garden
by the bed of poppies on the northwest slope, wind
in the trees and the five-mile sky billowing over us,
I am caught again by their colour: water-colour,
sheer, like ice or silk, or, we imagine,
freedom. Their petals on the ground
collect in drifts, explosions
of arterial light.
                    Or perhaps it's that we are
that membrane, an instant thick, days
shine right through us as we charge around,
looking for some explanation in what hasn't happened yet
or what will never happen again. Like last night at dinner:
glancing up at the picture, the one that's always hung there,
the sudden clear presentiment that I would live
to walk into that dining room someday, after
the last death, and find it
waiting for me, the entire past
dangling from a finishing nail.

Poppies, what can they teach us?
The windshot light fills them
and they are blind.

Recovery

And when at last grief has dried you out, nearly
weightless, like a little bone, one day,
no reason in particular, the world decides to tug:
twinge under the breastbone, the sudden thought
you might stand up, walk to the door and
keep on going . . . And in the seconds following,
like the silence following the boom under the river ice, it all
seems possible, the egg-smooth clarity of the new-awakened,
rising, to stand, and walk . . . But already
at the edges of the crack, sorrow
starts to ooze, the brown stain spreading
and you think: there is no end to it.

But in the breaking, something else is given — not
that glittering jumble, shrieking and churning in the blind
                              centre of the afternoon,
but something else — a scent,
like a door flung open, a sudden downpour
through which you can still see the sun, derelict
in the neighbour's field, the wren's bright eye in the thicket.
As though on that day in August, or even July,
when you were first thinking of autumn, you remembered also
the last day of spring, which had passed
without your noticing. Something that easy, let go
without a thought, untroubled by oblivion,
a bird, a smile.

Shade

. . . plants actually emit light . . . for a short time at the moment of change from light to darkness.

— *Plant and Planet*, Anthony Huxley

is not dusk, though it is often then
I think of it: the grape-hung oak
and hickory and maple trees
paused after the day's heat,
motionless. Nor is it shadow — something
a little sad, subtracted-from, where other
things get lost. Shadow is
what lengthens into dusk, the exhausted image of the world
laid out across itself. Shade
goes straight down, espresso,
dense with intent. And yet
it's not as though shade isn't what we think of
when we're tired.
         And as we learn from paintings,
shade is not mere absence, isn't black; and does
resemble shadow, being
many-coloured, subtle. So,
not single (though in this kind of heat
it feels like an embrace
to stretch out on the dark grass, breathe green
under the canopy, and doze) — shade is
multiple as leaves, each
cupping light, light spilling
over to the next, rilled, glinting,
until here, at the bottom,
it sways through the clearing, thick
as taffy; glossy, braided, sleek
               — but that's

the light; and shade
is other.
          Other,
then. Which is after all
a kind of absence, neither a
breathing out or breathing in, top
of the swing.
          Some place
where we are no one but ourselves
and in that moment of transition
give off light.

Beethoven: Op. 95

Nel mezzo del cammin di nostra vita
mi ritrovai per una selva oscura

I

An apology, first: I did not guess
the moodiness my middle years
would bring, unschooled as I was
in the varieties of frustration.
You were right: stupidity
surrounds us, and our own
splits the skull most sharply.
Also: that nothing
is achieved without the grimmest labour
on the slenderest of hopes
(except perhaps for Wolfgang, who was not
entirely human).
Not even music comes in its own words.

The importance of walks,
your duty to your nephew,
and the muscle in a true *cantabile*: you were right
about discipline, and politics,
the steep well of fury, and finally
what the fury goes through to: love
like a hand through the wall of the chest,
like a hand in fire, fire
tearing itself, in the hand's flame
a heart, in the heart's fist
an ear.

II

Remember this one?
Twenty-six miles he runs, in the sun,
Marathon to Athens, his heart
punching the blood through his lungs, runs
it will turn out — though he
won't live to know this — to announce
the dawning of the Golden Age.

The walls, and then the gate;
and the news that he has come
spreading before him like
the bright pool from a sacrifice, and still
he runs: to the agora,
to the Council Chamber, now
someone has recognized him and it's guessed
what news he brings; he slows — the crowd
behind him, shifting, tense — hauls
hugely on the air, roars *joy*,
we are victorious
and drops dead.

It's beside the point
the story is apocryphal. Myth is history
we need. And what matters is
the bit off camera,
not a goatherd or a guide car in sight,
around mile twenty, say, when the message
could be anything: the truth
has struck his body — *this*

cannot be done — but he takes
the next step anyway. Not out of loyalty
or pride, but because he is a runner,
and he wills it. And what matters is

some facts exhaust us this way, too.
We fight until the spirit's stripped,
nothing between us and the bare floor of the self, and then
the thing that cannot happen
happens, the thing that no one sees:
some place past emptiness
we take another step.

III

Hearing, you have reached the end,
the kernel bitter in your mouth.
Where would you go
even if your throat would open?
Only in the country,
relief (o, in the country!) — as if
every tree spoke.

If all comes to naught,
if all comes to naught . . .
All is coming to naught,
but the earth, sweet stillness,
remains, will remain. Woods,
hearing stillness, remain . . .

This plague, my hearing.
Only in the country, praise.
Only on the earth, sweetness.
Music, this sweetness,
deer in the twilight:
o hearing, o earth,
remain.

IV

A walk in autumn fields, the smell
of hay and dust not unlike
a canvas tent. In a year of downpours,
a week without rain: grasshoppers
bounce off through the weeds like coins.
A breeze in the blaze of aspens;
sun hums in the frozen sweep of spruce.

You are tired,
like the dry earth.
But unlike it
you know too much.
For still, that is
earth's definition:
whatever it knows,
that is enough.

And because it is fall,
darkness will shadow the northwest;
and because it is late in this century,
darkness will be in the air you breathe.
And because you are human, darkness
has come from your hand,
your mouth,
and it thickens around your heart
like fat around a liver: you will never
know enough.

            For you are alive:

here, sitting in the dirt,
the clumps of shorn alfalfa,
the crack in the dust,
hay down your collar, a wasp, the aspens
luminous, the luminous sky
big as an outflung arm.

For this is the world:
even you, with your hands, and your language,
and your fat black heart.

And the light,
the light shines on it.

V

And I misread the coda, too:
thought you thought
you'd heard some angel
clattering on the stairs.

But no.
The floundering, the rage, fistfuls
of wrong-shaped emptiness: you knew
as well as anyone.
God comes from the darkness —
if he comes —
like pain from a wound,
frost from concrete,
the next step.

Which is not to say
there is no joy — only that
it's never a reward.
That's all you meant:
the sweetest truth, or the most terrible,
can fly up, just like that, be lost
like dust in sunlight.

Beethoven: Op. 127, Adagio

I

Here at the end of summer
the heart talks to itself,
a thin stream braiding
over a lip of rock.

To go through a wall, then another —
galleries of silent, stone-ground light.
To go through, to that third room on the other side,
to empty the forest of your thoughts, the forest of your lungs,
this is where the heart goes in late summer,
the empty forest. Even the sunlight is alone.

In the third room, the heart sits on the floor
talking to itself. A little stream,
braiding over a lip of rock.
It is saying what it has said
from the beginning, no doors, no windows,
if anyone could hear.

II

The rise of the rib-cage,
      its fall: how unlikely this slight

shift of fabric. A tea cup,
      a music box.

Air enters, air flows away:
      how this simple thing

goes on and on, cannot
      help itself, on and on.

A-flat: cream's richness,
      like a good field in April, a blackness
            you wanted to eat,

or in August, the string's breath thick
      with heat and dust, like
            being able to breathe weight,

stooking, to have felt the chest thicken with brightness,
      as though light were substance, as though it
            carried the dark field inside itself, gleaming
                  to have breathed that brightness, have become

weight, that roll of hills
      their brocade of wheat and barley.
            To have lifted to the horizon

like earth, fallen
      like a rib-cage, stillness,

a long bright sigh of dust.

Absence

When the sky is no longer a roof
one's eyes are finally open:
it is in the valley one draws breath.

The pines are so slender. They weave
gently, almost without noise,
pushed by currents that do not reach us here.

Now the cities are behind us,
and the wars. Lantern-light
streams from the solitary window.

What is past drifts up then
without effort: river-scent
at twilight, through the rubble of the day.

Lancey Meadows

*Needing cloth to dry themselves, and food, they came out into the ocean and over
wide expanses, away toward Wineland, up into the uninhabited country. Evil
can take away luck, so that one dies early.*
— Runic inscription, Ringerike, Norway

Late in May, the strait is filled with ice.
Across it, fifty miles away, a patch of sunlight
scrapes the edge of the plateau. You see the axe
glance off and sink itself in bone two fields away
before you hear a sound: that silence
is the coast of Labrador.

For a year or two, they must have faced it dry-eyed
every morning. And in the spring
the wind would still have chased itself
along the flanks of their sod huts.
It would have been at night that empty heartbeat
opened in them, billion-year-old granite
weeping up into their pillows, lightless,
groping for its name.

The View from the Kitchen Window

Should be always of a tree, or
trees. Home
needs to be high ground, that is,
secure, and so
a slope, too. Which need not be dramatic,
though water in the near or middle distance
is usually an asset and suggests
a steeper incline.
At the limit, of course, a horizon,
a line at once wild and perfect
like, say, the edge of the world:
a ragged tear of muskeg spruce:
wrack of invisible
clear air.

April

How the light is sad.
How it will not leave us alone.
How we are tugged up staircases
by the way it angles across landings.
Or just our faces — tipped
to the clear, depleted sky.
How, because of sunset, the imagination
headquarters in the west.

Spring in the north: all that
tawny grass and gravel and nothing
green to sop up the excessive honesty.

Outside our windows,
something like youth or promises.
How the wind blows right through them,
blossoming. Fleet.

Rain Shadow

And in the late afternoon, after so much,
to come off the high plateau.
Who doesn't secretly love the Sahara?
The desert is a promise — that clean sweep
leaning out of the future,
one table and a single chair.
To abandon the heart, too,
with the other useless machines
and make the body empty as sky.
Which is always leaving
— and the hills, drifting in with sage
year after year, bearing it somehow.
It's this we'd like to be free of, this being
always on the brink:
the spring on the porch door creaks,
someone, you're sure,
about to speak to you, you're turning.

If we knew why we had come.
If we knew why we loved it anyway.

Highway 879

North out of the Sweetgrass Hills, their mass
fixed and improbable in my rearview mirror
the better part of an hour. Sunday,
near-record heat in April, he is asleep
beside me in the front seat.
The air is hazy with evaporating ice, still
you can see for thirty miles:
sheds, dugouts, the gridlock
of stubble and summerfallow, windbreaks
paralleling the section lines, and the road
like some edict of connection,
empty.

       Until
that coulee — the highway
dipping for a moment into olive-velvet shadow
and emerging
changed: the way two people
exhausted by a hard winter can make love
in the late afternoon and wake
to find the clutter of their lives no more than
a few already-leaning fenceposts under wind.
It is that easy to be happy.
Or unhappy. Vastness itself
a singularity.

You Must Believe in Spring

Because it is the garden. What is left to us.
Because silence is not silence without sound.
Because you have let the cat out, and then in, and then out,
       and then in, and then out, and then in, and then
       out, and then in, and then out, and then in,
       enough.
Because otherwise their precision at the blue line would
      mean nothing.
Because otherwise death would mean nothing.
Because the light says so.
Because a human being can gladly eat only so much cabbage.
Because the pockets of your overcoat need mending.
Because it's easy not to.
Because your sweaters smell.
Because Gregory of Nazianzen said geometry has no place in
      mourning, by which he meant despair presumes too
      much.
Because it ain't over 'til it's over. — Hank Aaron, Jackie
      Robinson. Satchel Paige.
Because Kant was wrong, and Socrates, Descartes and all the
      rest. Because it is the body thinking and Newt
      Gingrich would like you not to.
Because the signs are not wrong: you are here.
Because I love you. Or you love someone. Because someone
      is loved.
Because under the sun, everything is new.
Because the wet snow in the trees is clotted light.
Because in 1841 it took six cords of wood to get through a
      winter in one room at Harvard and two-thirds
      of Maine used to be open country as a result.

Because sleeping is not death.

Because although an asshole was practising his Elvis Presley
    imitation, full voice, Sunday morning, April 23rd
    at Spectacle Lake Provincial Park, the winter wren
    simply moved 200 yards down the trail.

Because the wren's voice is moss in sunlight, because it is
    a stream in sunlight over stones.

Because Beethoven titled the sonata.

I mean: would Bill Evans *and* Frank Morgan lie to you?

Because even sorrow has a source.

For, though it cannot fly, the heart is an excellent clamberer.

Lilacs

Restless, I walk out in the evening
to the old house; to the patio around the back
where the old lilacs bloom.
This is a surprise, for I would have said
I do not like this place, would not
come to it by choice:
the peeling lattice on the south side,
the crumbling cinder blocks that once made
a failed sort of fireplace on the east.
The pad was small, but even so
you have to pick your feet up not to stumble
where the concrete cracked.

The lilacs lean across the south-east corner,
blocking the walk.
If you asked my sister, she would say
it never happened, but I remember that
one spring we tamed a bumble-bee
when it came in the afternoons to feed.
She denies this now, of course,
or would; refuses any salvage, claims I'm inventing
if I say there were moments when the sun came out
like her hair in the shadows of the leaves, heavy, like cream, cut
blunt as a spoon, her small teeth
as she laughed up at me, the bee
humming in my palm as she stroked it; and though I
think hope may be a better guide to the past than despair

I now doubt, too — these lilacs
are probably thick with insects in the afternoons, it's

ridiculous to think we might have sat inside them safe,
you'd have to be careful, merely brushing by,
not to be stung. When you think of it
she must be right, because why else
would she deny it, and I bury my face
as I might imagine leaning into sea-foam:
cool, explosive; the way her hand
when it touched me could unlock the bone under its skin,
or how the drowned must feel,
rising through themselves from the ocean floor.

Driving Northwest

Driving Northwest in July before
the long twilight that stretches into
the short summer dark, despite the sun
the temperature is dropping, air
slips by the truck, like diving,
diving,
        and you are almost blind
with light: on either side of you
it floats across the fields, young barley
picking up the gold, oats white,
the cloudy bruise of alfalfa
along the fencelines, the air itself
tawny with haydust, and the shadows of the willows
in the draw miles long, oh it is lovely
as a myth, the touch of a hand on your hair,
and you need, like sleep, to lie down now
and rest, but you are almost
blind with light, the highway
stretched across the continent
straight at the sun: visor,
dark glasses, useless against its gonging,
the cab drowns in it, shuddering, you cannot tell,
you might be bleeding or suffocating, shapes
fly out of it so fast there's no time to swerve:
but there is no other path, there is no other bed,
it is the only way home you know.

Passing Sangudo

Sangudo, of the long hill and
the river flats; of the long shadows
in the river valley; Sangudo,
of the early evening, in the summertime,
on the way out Highway 43 after
a day in the city: how ugly
I used to think your name; and how,
unhappy in the car, unhappy
at the prospect of unwelcome dressed as welcome
that awaited us, I believed,
as we all believe, that growing up
meant never having to come back;
how, much though I deplored our town,
I was glad it wasn't you: that much smaller,
that much shabbier, the mud a little deeper,
the store fronts just that much more stark.
It must have rained most days that we drove past
because it rained most days then — or so it seems;
but of course plenty of times it must
have been winter, it being winter most of the year then
— or so it seems. And indeed the one recurring
nightmare of childhood, toboganning down the river bank
and falling through the ice, with my father for some reason,
as well as my sister, and all of us drowning, silently, the ice
growing rigid over us in jagged chunks — that winter dream
was set outside Sangudo, just where the highway
crosses the Pembina, twenty feet
downstream from the bridge.
So it is mildly surprising — like discovering, at 40,

your handwriting closely resembles your great-uncle's
though you've never met — surprising I should find
that what I remember now
is neither rain nor snow, but long shadows,
early summer twilight, the sweet forgiving
roll of the land, the car's movement through it
steady, a quiet humming, exactly as it should be,
coming from nowhere, destined nowhere, simply moving,
driving past Sangudo, over the dark brown Pembina,
up the long hill, home.

Trauermusik

In 1936, on the occasion of the death of King George V, Paul Hindemith, who was in London at the time giving a series of concerts, wrote a chamber work scored for string orchestra with viola solo. The fourth of its brief movements is a setting of the chorale "Vor deinen Thron tret' ich hiermit", known to most Lutherans as "Herr Gott, dich loben alle wir", and to most English-speaking church-goers as "Old Hundredth".

The melody is indeed old, among those Louis Bourgeois composed for the Genevan psalter in the mid-sixteenth century: its roots reach back, through the Dutch *Souter Liedekens*, into folksong. In Bach's harmonizations, as in Pachelbel's and others', the closing cadence is what music theorists call a perfect or authentic cadence — one in which a chord built on the fifth of the scale resolves to a chord built on the tonic. In a move you won't find described let alone recommended in the theory books, Hindemith, by contrast, writes a cadence that turns on an inverted triad on the sixth — and thereby manages to avoid sounding what musicians call the leading note. What is remarkable about this is not that there aren't plenty of standard cadences in which the leading note doesn't occur; it's that here, none of those standard cadences are available. The melody — that simple descending scale in the last two bars — together with the rules of classical harmony conspire to give the composer little leeway: they make a cadence that includes the leading note so overwhelmingly obvious that deciding not to use it is a bit like not using the Lion's Gate Bridge when you're in Stanley Park and want to get home to North Vancouver.

Those who have seen Ansel Adams' early photographs of the Golden Gate before its own bridge was built may have encountered a similar effect: although the landscape in those photographs is breathtakingly beautiful, and intact, and although that is surely the point, the imagination, conditioned by years of photographs since the bridge, senses that something is missing. The bridge, less necessary to what the Golden Gate *is* than the headlands of either the San Francisco or Marin Peninsulas, has nonetheless become definitive: it embodies one shape of human desire.

So, too, the leading note — the seventh in the eight-note scale. It gets its name because, more than any other, it tends to be followed by the tonic. But it leads not only by proximity, it leads because its emotional gaze, more than that of any other note, is directed home: the seventh is the interval most coloured by desire, the point at which the key is stretched to its limit, at which the demand for return is most intense.

Grief, too, has to do with homesickness; and in the closing measures of *Trauermusik* we are told a little of what this is. A cadence in which the leading note is not included — but in which our ear must detect its absence — says that mourning requires an acknowledgement that death is the absence of desire, that death moves with the indifference of the sunlight in these sunlit blocks of chords.

And, it tells us, in the relinquishing that is the end of mourning, we must pass through — as through a ghost — that absence in ourselves.

Acknowledgements

My sincere thanks to the Canada Council for its support from May 1993 to May 1994, during which time a number of these poems were written. My sincere thanks also to the literary presses and journals that first published them: *Brick* 53 (*"Trauermusik"*), *Descant* 84 & 88 ("Kant and Bruckner", "Beethoven: Op. 95", "Beethoven: Op. 127, Adagio"), *Edmonton Stroll of Poets* 1993 ("Driving Northwest"), *The Fiddlehead* 196 ("Cashion Bridge"), *Grain* 23/4 ("Bill Evans: 'Here's That Rainy Day'", "You Must Believe in Spring", "Transparence", "Absence", "Lancey Meadows"), *The Malahat Review* 105 & 111 ("Bartók's Roumanian Dances", "Open Strings", "Adagio, K. 219", "Brahms' Clarinet Quintet in B Minor, Op. 115", "Musicians", "Lilacs", "Border Station"), *Mānoa* 10/2 ("Highway 879"), *Nimrod* 37/2 ("Recovery", "Rain Shadow"), *Poetry Canada Review* 12/2 ("Five Songs for Relinquishing the Earth", "Passing Sangudo"), *Prism International* 33/4 ("April", "Shade", "Bill Evans: Alone"), *Proserpine Press* 1 ("The View from the Kitchen Window"), *Writing Home: A PEN Canada Anthology* ("Poppies"). And my thanks to the editors of *Windhorse Reader*, *Orbis* (U.K.), and *Rec* (Belgrade) for their interest in reprinting some of them.

For the time and advice that made the first edition possible, much gratitude to Linda Brine and Sally McKay. For the interest and support that made this one possible, equal gratitude to my co-editors at Brick.

"Open Strings" and "Musicians" are for members of the New Brunswick Chamber Orchestra, as that group existed in the spring of 1992. "Cashion Bridge" is for Charles Barbour.

This book is for Don McKay.